Prayer Secrets
Four Keys to Results

by Susan Sherwood Parr

Published by

WORD PRODUCTIONS

wordproductions.org • prayerworkshop.com

Published by
Word Productions LLC
Since 1979
www.wordproductions.org
www.prayerworkshop.com

Available at bookstores,
and most online bookstores.

Dedication

To My Mother, a godly example
and inspiration to me all of my life...

"Thank You, Mom."

Contents

Key One

Consecration to God

Getting Started

The Adventure Begins

Be anxious for nothing, but in everything by prayer and supplication, with thanksgiving, let your requests be made known to God.   —Philippians 4:6

Through this book, you will become renewed in your excitement for spiritual things and in your excitement about God Himself, His faithfulness, and the integrity of His Word. You are going to receive answers to your prayers. Through spending time with God in prayer, you will experience the priceless treasure of developing a relationship with God.

For many years I prayed, but something was missing. I'm going to share that missing element with you in *Prayer Secrets.* This missing element drastically changed my prayer life forever. It will also change yours. After people accept Jesus as their personal Savior and Lord, they are then enabled, through grace, to begin a close relationship with God. Prayer and communion with God will cause you to have such a relationship with God. I promise that as you engage in the adventure of prayer, you will never be the same again.

Prayer need not be tedious. God does not require you to perform a list of prerequisites before He will answer you. Yet there are things that God asks of us.

This bit of advice from the apostle Paul sums it up: Don't worry; instead, pray about everything. His words then add that the peace of God, which surpasses understanding, will keep our hearts and minds through Christ Jesus. What a promise! Of course, we must pray according to God's will and in line with what Scripture teaches us, but there are many things we can pray for that are God's will.

In the Old Testament, David prayed that God would overthrow the works of darkness, and in response God sent out His arrows and scattered the foe, with lightning in abundance, and He vanquished them (Psalm 18:14). There are many answers to personal prayers in the Bible.

First Things First: Forgive

Before you pray, you need to be sure there is nothing between you and God. First John 1:9 teaches us that if we confess our sins, He is faithful and just to forgive us and cleanse us from all unrighteousness.

You need to ask for forgiveness of your sins. You also need to forgive others of anything you have against them. How can we ask for forgiveness if we refuse to forgive others their trespasses against us (Luke 6:37, 17:3)? If I feel like I can't forgive, I ask for the Lord's help: "God, I can't forgive, but I ask You to love and forgive in and through me by Your Holy Spirit. Please give me the grace." This will work!

Leave your gift there before the altar, and go your way. First be reconciled to your brother, and then come and offer your gift. Matthew 5:24

Hindrances to Answered Prayer

Look at the list of hindrances to prayer below. Take time to pray about these issues in your life. Once you've done it, you will be more likely to recognize these things as hindrances in your walk with God. You will want to take each issue to God, removing these obstacles from your life as soon as possible.

Here are some of the enemies and road-blocks to answered prayer:

- Unforgiveness (Matthew 5:23–24)
- Hatred (John 2:11)
- Doubt (Matthew 21:21; Mark 9:14–29)
- Fear (Matthew 14:30)
- Unconfessed sin (Isaiah 59:2)

Steps to Freedom

1. Confess. After you examine yourself, ask God to forgive and cleanse you:

> *If we confess our sins, He is faithful and just to forgive us our sins and to cleanse us from all unrighteousness.* 1 John 1:9

2. Accept forgiveness and cleansing. Walk in faith with a conscience void of offense toward God.

> *Let us draw near with a true heart in full*

assurance of faith, having our hearts
sprinkled from an evil conscience and
our bodies washed with pure water.
Hebrews 10:22

Noted University Study

Below is an excerpt from *Stanford Medicine,*
summer 1999, published by Stanford
University Medical Center.

The Art and Science of Forgiveness

If you feel good but want to feel even
better, try forgiving someone.
By Frederic Luskin, Ph.D.

For centuries, the world's religious
and spiritual traditions have
recommended the use of forgiveness
as a balm for hurt or angry feelings.
Psychotherapists have worked to
help their clients to forgive, and

some have written about the importance of forgiveness. Until recently,
however, the scientific literature has
not had much to say about the effect
of forgiveness. But that's starting to
change. While the scientific study of
forgiveness is just beginning—the rel-
evant intervention research having
been conducted only during the past
ten years—when taken together, the
work so far demonstrates the power
of forgiveness to heal emotional
wounds and hints that forgiveness
may play a role in physical healing
as well.

What is intriguing about this
research is that even people who are
not depressed or particularly anxious
can obtain the improved emotional
and psychological functioning that
comes from learning to forgive. This
suggests that forgiveness may enable

people who are functioning adequately to feel even better. Published studies on forgiveness have shown the importance of forgiveness training on coping with a variety of psychologically painful experiences. Studies have been conducted with adolescents who felt neglected by their parents, with women who were abused as children, with elderly women who felt hurt or uncared for, with males who disagreed with their female partners' decisions to have abortions, and with college students who had been hurt. These studies showed that when given forgiveness training of varying lengths and intensities, participants could become less hurt and become more able to forgive their offenders.

Receive Forgiveness

Forgiving others is powerful. According to the above study, receiving forgiveness brings emotional and physical benefits to the forgiver's life. It also can benefit the lives of those being forgiven. Perhaps there can now be the opportunity for healing in a severed relationship in your life.

Forgiveness gives us a clear conscience and peace of mind. "Forgive and be forgiven" is good advice.

The Missing Element

So, what was the element missing in my praying? I'm not going to share that until I build a foundation. Hopefully, as you wait for the secret, you will only become more excited about your new adventure with God in prayer, but will begin to spend some time each day with your Lord.

Key Two

Ask According to God's Will

The Integrity of God's Word
God and His Word Are One!

In the beginning was the Word, and the Word was with God, and the Word was God.   —John 1:1

Just think of it: Our God is the almighty, limitless God, who loves us so much that He sent His only begotten Son to die for our sins. Jesus satisfied the requirement of an atonement for our sins by His death on the cross. He was the Lamb of God. No longer do we need to sacrifice a lamb for our sins, because Jesus, the Messiah promised in the Old Testament, has come.

We *Can* Trust in God

Throughout the Bible, and in the experience of every Christian, God's integrity is confirmed. What does the Bible say about His integrity? Numbers 23:19 says,

God is not a man that He should lie...
Has He said, and will He not do?
Or has He spoken, and will He not
make it good?

In the New Testament, Paul said, "All the promises of God in Him are Yes, and in Him Amen, to the glory of God through us" (2 Corinthians 1:20).

God never lies. God is true, which means He is faithful to fulfill His promises to us. If you could think about trusting anyone on the face of the earth or in heaven, it would have to be God. We can trust in God. His Word will never return void.

As the rain comes down, and the snow
from heaven, and do not return there,
but water the earth, and make it bring

forth and bud, that it may give seed to the sower and bread to the eater, so shall my Word be that goes forth from my mouth; It shall not return to Me void, but it shall accomplish what I please, and it shall prosper in the thing for which I sent it. Isaiah 55:10–11

According to God's Will

A Step Toward Results

❧

Now this is the confidence that we have in Him, that if we ask anything according to His will, He hears us.
—1 John 5;14

Whether you are a beginner or a prayer warrior, here is a mini-workshop to teach you or refresh your mind on the steps to powerful prayer. Follow these steps one by one and you will see a change in your prayer life:

1. Confess your sins to God (1 John 1:9).

2. List your requests. "Let your requests be made known to God" (Philippians 4:6). Making a list helps you to remember

you have prayed about things. During a quiet time with the Lord, you can take out that list and thank Him for what He is doing about each of the requests. Thanking Him for what He is doing is actively showing faith. This pleases God (Hebrews 11:6).

3. You can pray as David: "Let them be ashamed and brought to mutual confusion who seek to destroy my life; let them be driven backward and brought to dishonor who wish me evil" (Psalm 40:14). When a spiritual battle is going on in your life or in the life of someone you know, praying this way brings great results. God is limitless and you can know and experience His power in your own prayer life.

4. Pray in detail. Make specific (scriptural) requests to the Father in Jesus's name. You can always add "if it be Your will" to the end of a prayer if you don't

know the will of God. Please note that although I am teaching on specific requests, and not to be selfish. God cares about your individual needs and wants you to pray about them, the variety and scope of your praying can be limitless. In our prayer group, when we have prayed for one serious need, God has led us to pray for a whole congregation about the same need or even to pray around the world.

5. Place your trust in God's specific promises. Know that this trust is faith in who God is, in His integrity, and in the integrity of the Word in which we rest our faith.

6. Thank God and praise Him for what He is doing. "By prayer and supplication, with thanksgiving, let your requests be made known to God" (Philippians 4:6).

What Does God Do?

God is faithful. His promises are true (1 Corinthians 1:20). His Word is true (Romans 3:4). He will watch over His Word to perform it (Isaiah 55:11).

Would you like to have a prayer life that brings results? What I would like to do is to teach you to become a prayerful person who is consecrated to God. Put God and His Word first and you will see that God is alive and that He hears and answers scriptural prayer today!

Things That Are God's Will

If you need to pray according to God's will, what sorts of things can you pray about? If you want to know what God's will is, here are some things that are *always* His will:

1   Salvation (Mark 16:16)

2.   Forgiveness of sins (1 John 1:9)

3.   Receiving God's grace (Romans 5:1–24)

4. Miracles and healing, according to His will (1 Corinthians 12:28)

5. Deliverance from evil, that is, helping to restore the damage caused by sins and circumstances (Jeremiah 3:22; Psalm 103:3; 107:20; Matthew 4:24; James 5:16)

6. Healing relationships where human will is open (Luke 4:18)

7. Protection from evil (Psalm 91)

8. Supplying needs (Philippians 4:19)

9. Leading by the Holy Spirit (Romans 8:14)

10. Wisdom and understanding (James 1:5) (Matthew 6:10; Philippians 2:13)

You can see that there are a large number of things you can ask for in prayer. Look at it like going on an adventure—a prayer adventure. Praying according to God's will is easy and fun. It's fun because He always answers prayers for things that are already

His will. His timing is perfect. He may not answer us when or in the way we think He should, but He will definitely come through at the perfect time.

Results come when we pray scripturally and when we rest on Him and His specific promises. Thank Him for the answer in advance. That's faith. Faith pleases God (Hebrews 11:6). There are many types of prayer, and we will cover some of them in this lesson. This will be an overview and not an in-depth study.

Key Three

Rest Your Faith in God
AND HIS PROMISES

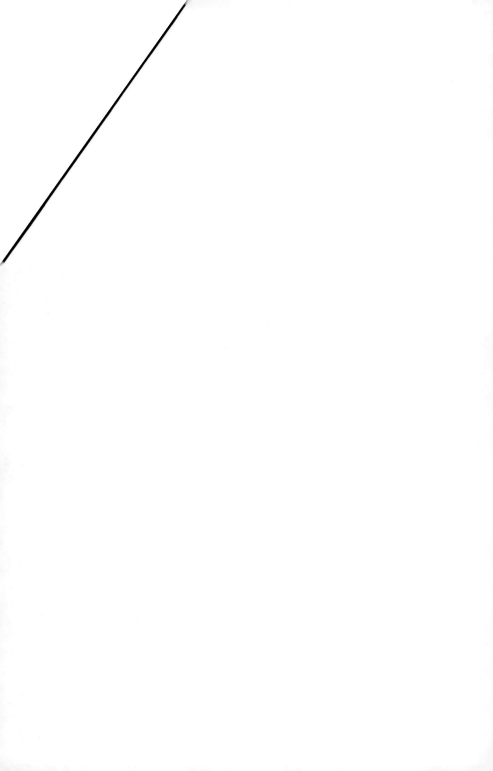

4

The Missing Element

Prayer Secret

For all the promises of God in Him are Yes, and in Him Amen, to the glory of God through us.   —1 Cor. 1:20

If you cheated and looked ahead to find out the secret, that's okay! I probably would have done the same thing if I were reading this book for the first time. I was guilty of doing that another time in my life.

Some years ago, I had been hurt badly by a person and found myself in a depression. I raced to the Christian bookstore in the little town I was living in at the time, found a book on coming out of depression, and thumbed through the pages to get to the answer I needed. I didn't want to hear a bunch of stories about people who were depressed; I just wanted the answer.

When I found it, I put it into practice. This Bible teacher simply said that thanking God was the answer.

I started to put that approach into practice although I didn't feel like it. My healing took place over a number of months. I gradually came out of it.

Since that time, I have found keys that bring faster results. I am amazed by God's power when we go to Him correctly.

The Missing Element Revealed

There was indeed a missing element in all of the time I had been spending in prayer. I knew about praying in Jesus's name, casting my cares on Him, and thanking Him for the answer. But sometimes I had an uneasiness or hard-to-explain feeling. I just couldn't be sure God really had my faith and heart.

What made the difference? Believe me, there is indeed a difference. There was one key element missing from my prayers. Some events took place in my life that led me to the missing ingredient.

While in Bible college, I made a decision that I would seek the face of God. My plan was to spend as much time as I could with God in prayer and in His Word. The Scriptures say that if we seek Him, we will find Him (Isaiah 45:19), and that He is a rewarder of those who diligently seek Him (Hebrews 11:6).

From the stories in the Bible, I had determined that if anyone spent time with God, he or she would be transformed. I somehow thought that if I spent enough time, I would be saturated with God's glory, presence, and grace and be transformed to the point where I would easily know His voice or will. I was excited at the prospect of such closeness to God. I began my quest. Strangely enough, instead of feeling marvelous or feeling like God's presence flooded my life, I felt terrible.

I was going through spiritual battles and certainly didn't feel holy, spiritual, or bathed in God's presence. What was wrong? I was really confused about it all.

I finished another day of classes and then dropped in on a friend. On her coffee table was a small booklet by a pastor's wife (I don't remember the title). I reached down, picked it up, and started to read a random page that basically told the following story:

As a pastor's wife, the author had been going through one of the most trying times of her life. She felt miserable, and it seemed that nothing she did helped. Finally she realized that she had been praying and praying, but in a random manner. She prayed, "I turn this over to You, Lord. Take care of this."

She discovered that the one thing she hadn't tried was to find specific Scriptures to stand on and place her confidence in.

She became specific in her prayers, relying on specific promises, and she prayed to the Father in Jesus's name. Finally, she thanked God for what He was doing. She did it and everything changed.

Was This It?

There it was! My answer was in that little booklet. I went home, sat on the floor in front of the coffee table with a pencil and a piece of paper, and got started. I made a detailed list of requests. I wrote down every need I could think of. When you do this, you can write down physical, emotional, and every other kind of need. I had four pages of stuff. I figured that since this was going to work, I might as well cover everything I knew or knew about.

A Nugget of Gold

When I finished praying, I was amazed! Not only did I feel peace inside of my heart, but to my utter joy, I felt total peace in my mind. I had discovered a nugget of gold on that afternoon. I was rewarded for seeking God, all right. I had received a treasure that would change my life forever.

On another occasion I heard a Bible teacher on the radio teach about prayer. He had said to make a list. The precept was that to write it down was to remember. Then he said to go to the Father in Jesus's name, take authority over the enemy, make one's requests known to God, and thank Him for the answers.

I kept my list with me, thanking God over each request in my devotional time. When I felt troubled, I remembered my prayer list and thanked God for what He was doing. Answers began.

It's funny how we either forget what we prayed about or we forget to pray at all about some things. Maybe we are lazy, pre-occupied, or just plain discouraged.

Or maybe we never knew God would answer our prayers in the here and now. Do a search in the Bible. See how many places you can find where someone prayed and God answered.

Writing requests in a journal helps us remember precisely what we have prayed for. This helps us to walk in faith (which pleases God). Thanksgiving is not only obedience to Philippians 4:6, but it also demonstrates faith toward God.

5

Kinds of Prayer

The Excitement Heightens

Be anxious for nothing, but in everything by prayer and
supplication, with thanksgiving, let your requests be
made known to God;   —Philippians 4:6

Ephesians 6:18 tells us to pray always with
all prayer and supplication in the Spirit.
What does "all prayer" include? It includes
thanksgiving, praise, worship, prayer in the
Spirit, supplication, and standing on specific
promises (the Amplified Bible describes it
as resting the whole of our confidence and
trust on God).

In this chapter we will cover a few of the
many types of prayer. In its basic sense, it is
communication or conversation with God.

Intercession

In Genesis 18, Abraham talked (prayed) to God. He interceded and asked God to spare Sodom and Gomorrah if he could find a certain number of righteous people. This was intercession, which is going to God on behalf of another person or situation. Intercessory prayer has a number of methods, all of which are the Holy Spirit working through the intercessor. First, it is the simple form mentioned above. Second, the intercessor will pray for a person or situation until the intercessor knows he or she is done. Third, it is a "work of prayer" that may take a long time, where the intercessor will be called upon to pray for the same person or situation whenever led by the Holy Spirit until the intercessor knows he or she is finished with the task.

We may not know exactly how to pray, but the Holy Spirit knows. We can rely on the Holy Spirit to lead us in prayer.

Seeking the Face of God

In 2 Chronicles 7:14, God tells His people what to do to be spared from judgment: "If My people who are called by My name will humble themselves, and pray and seek My face, and turn from their wicked ways, then I will hear from heaven, and will forgive their sin and heal their land." Here are other examples of seeking God:

You will seek the LORD your God, and you will find Him if you seek Him with all your heart and with all your soul.
Deuteronomy 4:29

Seek the LORD and His strength; Seek His face evermore!
1 Chronicles 16:11

In the sight of all Israel, the assembly of the LORD, and in the hearing of our God, be careful to seek out all the commandments of the LORD your God, that you

may possess this good land, and leave it
as an inheritance for your children after
you forever. 1 Chronicles 28:8

[Azariah] went out to meet Asa, and
said to him: "Hear me, Asa, and all
Judah and Benjamin. The LORD is with
you while you are with Him. If you seek
Him, He will be found by you; but if you
forsake Him, He will forsake you."
2 Chronicles 15:2

Seeking God should be a regular part of
our Christian lives. We need to remain close
to Him. He is our life and the strength of
our lives (Psalm 27). Here is an example of
not seeking God: "[Rehoboam] did evil,
because he did not prepare his heart to seek
the LORD" (2 Chronicles 12:14).

Worship and Praise
Second Chronicles 20:12–22 tells the story
of the prophet Jahaziel. The Spirit of the

Lord told him to tell the people not to be afraid of the great multitude that was coming against them. It was the Lord's battle and not theirs. When they began to sing and to praise, the Lord caused an ambush against their enemies. This is an exciting example of what God can do when we look to Him, worship Him, and praise Him!

[King Jehoshaphat said:] "O our God, will You not judge them? For we have no power against this great multitude that is coming against us; nor do we know what to do, but our eyes are upon You." Now all Judah, with their little ones, their wives, and their children, stood before the LORD.

Then the Spirit of the LORD came upon Jahaziel the son of Zechariah, the son of Benaiah, the son of Jeiel, the son of Mattaniah, a Levite of the sons of Asaph, in the midst of the assembly. And he said, "Listen, all you of Judah

and you inhabitants of Jerusalem, and
you, King Jehoshaphat! Thus says the
LORD to you: 'Do not be afraid nor dis-
mayed because of this great multitude,
for the battle is not yours, but God's.
Tomorrow go down against them. They
will surely come up by the Ascent of Ziz,
and you will find them at the end of the
brook before the Wilderness of Jeruel.
You will not need to fight in this battle.
Position yourselves, stand still and see
the salvation of the LORD, who is with
you, O Judah and Jerusalem!' Do not
fear or be dismayed; tomorrow go out
against them, for the LORD is with you."

And Jehoshaphat bowed his head with
his face to the ground, and all Judah
and the inhabitants of Jerusalem bowed
before the LORD, worshiping the LORD.
Then the Levites of the children of the
Kohathites and of the children of the
Korahites stood up to praise the LORD

God of Israel with voices loud and high.

So they rose early in the morning and went out into the Wilderness of Tekoa; and as they went out, Jehoshaphat stood and said, "Hear me, O Judah and you inhabitants of Jerusalem: Believe in the LORD your God, and you shall be established; believe His prophets, and you shall prosper." And when he had consulted with the people, he appointed those who should sing to the LORD, and who should praise the beauty of holiness, as they went out before the army and were saying:

"Praise the LORD, for His mercy endures forever."

Now when they began to sing and to praise, the LORD set ambushes against the people of Ammon, Moab, and Mount Seir, who had come against Judah; and they were defeated.

Prayer of the Spirit

When we pray in the Spirit, the Holy Spirit takes over, praying through us according to God's will. The following Scriptures mention this kind of prayer:

> *The Spirit … helps in our weaknesses. For we do not know what we should pray for as we ought, but the Spirit Himself makes intercession for us with groanings which cannot be uttered.*
> Romans 8:26

> *You, beloved, building yourselves up on your most holy faith, praying in the Holy Spirit …* Jude 20

Waiting in the Presence of God

I have found waiting in the presence of God to be a type of prayer that always brings results.

While I was attending Bible college, one of my teachers was an intercessor. During one of his classes, he told us that the most powerful and greatest kind of prayer was waiting in the presence of God on behalf of someone or some situation. He said he didn't know why it was so powerful, but his experience had proven it to be so. I listened and wondered.

"Mom" Goodwin

I left class that day to drive to Mom Goodwin's house. "Mama," as I called her, was my spiritual mother. She was living in Broken Arrow, Oklahoma, at the time. She had moved there after her husband went home to be with the Lord. She and her husband, Rev. J. R. Goodwin, were pastors for forty-eight years in the Assemblies of God churches and were written about in John Sherrill's book *They Speak with Other Tongues.* They knew about the moving of the Holy Spirit.

Mom had a ministry of intercession. She would have an experience, dream, or word of knowledge, then pray about it. In the next few days she would see what she prayed about on the news or in the lives of those they ministered to. She and J. R. were known for their counseling ministry to ministers.

Frequently, I went to her house to fix her hair, clean her house, cook a meal, or enjoy fellowship and prayer. We spent many hours together. My association with Mom Goodwin was a special blessing to my life. (I will use fictional names for my other friends in the story.)

I continued driving to Mom Goodwin's house, and twice these thoughts came to mind: "Jennie and John can't get out of the Middle East. If someone would wait in God's presence on their behalf, God could get them out of the country." Mind you, I didn't know they couldn't get out of Jordan. John was from Jordan. He and Jennie had married and gone to visit his family.

I pulled into the driveway, got out of the car, and walked up to the door where Mom

Goodwin met me. Before I even stepped inside, she said these words: "Susan, I just got a call from Voralee [Jennie and I used to rent from her while in Bible school], and she got a letter from Jennie and they say they can't get out of the Middle East."

I said, "Mom, you won't believe what just happened while driving over here." I told her about the Bible teaching on prayer and about the thoughts that came to me on my way to her house.

"Honey, that sounds like God to me. You better do it."

I was excited. That night I sat in the presence of God on their behalf. I had sought the Lord many times, but this time I just sat there feeling foolish and wondering, *Should I read a Scripture? Do I do anything?* I pretty much just sat there in the presence of God, remembering part of Brother Lawrence's book *The Practice of the Presence of God.* But I didn't feel anything.

In two days I got word that my friends

had gained legal permission to leave the Middle East. While I know that others were praying too, I also know that God had moved when I waited in His presence.

The proof that my impression from God while driving was true came in the result. This was really God's Spirit speaking to me. Everything that God said would happen came to pass when I prayed as He directed me to pray.

The Next Year

Almost a year to the date, Jennie and John told me that John's brother couldn't get out of the Middle East. He wanted to come to the United States to go to school but had been turned down eleven times by Europe and the U.S.

The next morning I had a dream before waking: I felt an intense love in my heart. Then I heard myself speaking to John. "John, I will pray. God can get your brother out of the country." I awoke with that.

What will John think if I tell him that? What if that wasn't the Lord? I thought about it for quite a while with mixed feelings of excitement, wonder, and concern. I knew that God could do this. The experience was mixed with a tremendous amount of love and the knowledge that God had done it for my friends a year earlier. I decided that I would be careful how I said it, but that I would go and tell them that night.

"John," I began, "I'll pray. God can get your brother out of the country."

"Oh, thank you, Susie," he said.

That was it! I went home and did it. I spent about an hour waiting in God's presence. I also spent some time the next day, hoping to feel like I was done waiting in His presence for James's need. In two days, permission was granted for my friend's brother to come to the U.S.

Through this kind of prayer, God moves mountains, binds devils, overthrows the powers of darkness, sends His mighty heavenly armies, and subdues the enemy in the situation. I don't know why it is so powerful. Maybe part of it is just spending time with Him. He is high and lifted up; I am a helpless one coming to Him.

When all hope seems gone and you don't know what to do, wait in God's presence on behalf of the situation.

6

Miraculous Answers

God's Glory Revealed

∾∾

Call unto me, and I will answer thee, and shew thee
great and mighty things, which thou knowest not.
—Jeremiah 33:3

My son decided to take a trip to Spain with
just his backpack to "live off the land." I
prayed all the way through his absence, and
there were countless little miracles. Just
before he came back to this country, some
interesting things happened. Here is the
condensed version.

Two mornings in a row I was awakened
and felt led by the Holy Spirit to wait in
God's presence on my son's behalf. Each of
those days, I felt I should share specific

things with my son. For instance, my son wanted God to show him that Jesus was God. He didn't want to believe in Jesus just because he was raised in a Christian church; he wanted to know for himself that Jesus Christ is God.

I felt led to tell my son about an experience I had at about his age. It was a time when God caused deep feelings that clearly made me feel a certain direction was wrong. I had those intense feelings for almost a month. I couldn't figure it out because I had never had anything like that happen before. I didn't listen to the "don't do it" feelings, and I ended up in a bad situation. I told my son that this was the first time God had spoken to me that way and that I wished I had known it was God. I then told my son that I would trust his wisdom and asked him to be sensitive to his gut feelings.

The next morning I woke with the knowledge that I was to pray again. I felt like I should call my son. If I hadn't called him at that moment, I wouldn't have reached him. He was on a train headed toward France. He said, "Mom, I just wanted to tell you: It happened to me. I felt inside of me that I should come home. But I want to test it. Nothing like this has ever happened to me."

I thought, *Oh no. If God wants him home and he's headed toward France, now what?* I knew that he could be headed for trouble. Soon he was out of cell phone reach. I called a few of my prayer partners and asked them to pray, and then I went on to work.

The next morning I felt that I should try and call him one more time and that perhaps he was now in an area when he could be reached by cell phone.

God Speaks to My Son
Here is what had happened after my son had last talked to me.

He got off the train in France and found somewhere to sleep for the night. Waking, he had a feeling come over him that he couldn't do this anymore, that he was drained, and that this was the end of his trying to live off the land in Europe.

That was it! God spoke to my son even though he wasn't sure it was God. He got on a flight that stopped in Madrid on its way to New York. When I called him, he was indeed in calling range (his cell phone was only for Spain).

"Mom, I'm so glad you called me. I was hoping you would. I'm getting on a plane for the United States right now. In fact, if you had waited a minute, we would be taking off and you couldn't have gotten through to me." My son got on the plane and was soon back at work in the States.

God's Power Manifested in Loss

Another beautiful example of waiting in

God's presence took place in 2004.

It was four in the morning and my husband couldn't sleep. I was also stirring. I am an early morning person anyway. This is when I usually spend time with the Lord. I went downstairs and was ready to start my devotions when the phone rang.

It was a friend of mine calling from Michigan. "Jimmy is on life support. He's brain-dead and on a respirator. They're going stop using the respirator at 11:00 this morning."

I couldn't believe it! This is a young man our prayer group had been praying for. His father said that he had been experiencing sleep apnea and that he just stopped breathing.

I told him that I had gotten up to pray and would pray for Jimmy. I made a couple of calls to prayer partners and began to wait in God's presence.

Around six, I felt something in my heart that I couldn't explain. I didn't know what it meant, so I just remained before the Lord. I prayed a few different things as I waited, such as that God would send His angels to the hospital in Michigan, that He would pour out His Spirit, and that, if He could speak to Jimmy even in a coma, He would.

"Have mercy on him, Lord. Remember him as a child. I ask for Your kindness toward him. You are the only One who can help him. Please don't let him die without being ready." Those are basically all the prayers I could think of.

At 8:10 AM, John 11:25–26 came to my mind. "I am the resurrection and the life. He who believes in Me, though he may die, he shall live. And whoever lives and believes in Me shall never die." I didn't know what God was saying to me. I thought I'd start some housework, but then I felt strongly that God wanted me to stay before Him for Jimmy.

Next, from 8:15 to 8:30 AM, the most wonderful thing I've ever experienced happened to me. God poured out His powerful, supernatural presence upon me. I was filled with gratitude and worship. I was praising Him with a supernatural awareness of His goodness, kindness, and compassion. How wonderful God was to Jimmy! God was almighty—He was great! Jesus had filled my being. I wept with joy in the Spirit. It was a greater experience than I have ever yet enjoyed.

I knew Jimmy was okay. It was only thirty minutes till they were going to remove the respirator. I decided I should stay before the Lord until that time. At 11:00 Michigan time, a tremendous, silent presence of God came over me. I felt like a child. I thought Jesus and His angels must be ready to take Jimmy.

He was. As the respirator was removed from Jimmy, his dad holding his hand, Jimmy left this life... and stepped into glory with the Lord Jesus Christ.

7

Spiritual Warfare

"Lord, Fight Our Battles!"

The Lord will fight for you, and you shall hold your
peace."ou knowest not.   —Exodus 14:14

Spiritual warfare is something you will
become more aware of as you dig deeper
into the things of God. Until that happens
to you, life's obvious battles are what you
will think require spiritual warfare. Let me
tell you, it goes deeper than that.

I begin this chapter by making it clear
that where spiritual warfare is concerned,
there is no question in whom the victory
lies. It lies in Jesus Christ, in His power, and
in the power of God's Word.

Unless God specifically leads you to address the devil, don't. Keep your focus on God and on what He has called you to do.

Ask God to fight your spiritual battles in Jesus's name and trust in His power.

> *For we do not wrestle against flesh and blood, but against principalities, against powers, against the rulers of the darkness of this age, against spiritual hosts of wickedness in the heavenly places.* Ephesians 6:12

In this life we aren't playing games. There is a real battle going on. And God's Word is a spiritual weapon. In the book of Ephesians, when Paul is teaching the Body of Christ about their armor, he says,

> *Take the helmet of salvation, and the sword of the Spirit which is the Word of God; praying always with all prayer and supplication in the Spirit, being watchful to this end with all perseverance and supplication for all the saints.* Ephesians 6:17–18

Another biblical writer echoed Paul's sentiments about the power of God's Word as a weapon. "The Word of God is living and powerful, and sharper than any two-edged sword, piercing even to the division of soul and spirit, and of joints and marrow, and is a discerner of the thoughts and intents of the heart" (Hebrews 4:12).

Learn to Use the Sword

Learn to use the Word of God properly. The difference between improper application of the Word and its proper application is like the difference between children who play at sword fighting and a swordsman who, after much training, has developed his skill. The swordsman is a master at what he does. The muscles he uses have become developed and strong. He has become quick, and when he strikes with the sword, he hits his target forcefully.

It doesn't come overnight, but after much training, we become master swordsmen with the Word of God!

Jesus stood on Scripture when He faced temptation (Matthew 4). The very Word of God proceeded from His mouth.

The Word of God is the sword of the Spirit. Remember this vital part of Scripture: "praying always with all prayer and supplication in the Spirit" (Ephesians 6:18). Praying in the Spirit is a spiritual weapon.

There is power in the Word of God. It is spiritual food, and it is the sword of the Spirit. The enemy must flee in the name of Jesus, and God's Word is a weapon. "Having disarmed principalities and powers, He made a public spectacle of them, triumphing over them in it" (Colossians 2:15).

One example of prayer using the Sword of the Spirit follows:

Father, Your Word says in Psalm 27 that You are the strength of my life. I thank You for it! You are no respecter of

persons. Your Word says that You are
able to do more than I can ask or even
think. There is nothing too hard for You.
You are the mighty God, limitless in
power. Your Word will not return void! I
praise You for what you are doing in
my life.

Can you find the Scripture within the above prayer? There are seven mentioned in this prayer.

Jesus has already defeated Satan for you through His redemptive work of the cross. We make this a living reality through prayer and by the appropriation of God's promises for our own lives (2 Corinthians 10:4; 1 Peter 5:9).

Key Four

―――――― ❧ ――――――

Praise and Thank God
FOR WHAT HE IS DOING

.

8

Forget the Past

Look Forward

Brethren, I do not count myself to have apprehended; but one thing I do, forgetting those things which are behind and reaching forward to those things which are ahead... —Phil. 3:13–14

The first step toward your last key is to forget the past and look forward. Once, while meditating on the above verse, I had some interesting thoughts:

1. Forget the past.

2. Look forward.

3. Don't base anything from your past on what God will do in your future.

4. Don't think that He will work in your life the same way He has moved previously. He is a God of new things and the creator of things to come. He even says

that He will lead us in paths we have
not known and make the darkness as
light before us.

How can you forget the past? By God's
grace. What is grace? It is free, undeserved
favor or blessing. Here is what the Bible says
about the grace of God given to you when
you became a Christian:

*Having been justified by faith, we have
peace with God through our Lord Jesus
Christ, through whom also we have
access by faith into this grace in which
we stand, and rejoice in hope of the
glory of God.* Romans 5:1–2

*If by the one man's offense death
reigned through the one, much more
those who receive abundance of grace
and of the gift of righteousness will reign
in life through the One, Jesus Christ.*
Romans 5:17

*Of His fullness we have all received, and
grace for grace. For the law was given
through Moses, but grace and truth
came through Jesus Christ.*
John 1:16–17

Confirmation that this grace exists in
the Christian's life is found in the following
Scriptures:

*When [Barnabas] came and had seen
the grace of God, he was glad, and
encouraged them all that with purpose
of heart they should continue with the
Lord. Acts 11:23*

*Brethren, I commend you to God and to
the word of His grace, which is able to
build you up and give you an inheritance among all those who are sancti-
fied. Acts 20:32*

God Says to Forget the Past

God says, "Forget the past." Forget it! What God is doing is in front of you. Think about that for a moment. Thirty seconds ago doesn't exist anymore. Your whole future is in front of you. What God will and can do is ahead of you. What does the Bible say about this?

Paul said: "Not that I have already attained, or am already perfected; but I press on, that I may lay hold of that for which Christ Jesus has also laid hold of me."

> Brethren, I do not count myself to have apprehended; but one thing I do, forgetting those things which are behind and reaching forward to those things which are ahead, I press toward the goal for the prize of the upward call of God in Christ Jesus. Philippians 3:12–14

*God said: "I am the L*ORD*, your Holy*
One, the Creator of Israel, your King."
*Thus says the L*ORD*, who makes a way*
in the sea and a path through the
mighty waters, Who brings forth the
chariot and horse, the army and the
power (They shall lie down together,
they shall not rise; they are extinguished,
they are quenched like a wick.
"Do not remember the former things,
nor consider the things of old.
Behold, I will do a new thing, now it
shall spring forth; shall you not know it?
I will even make a road in the wilder-
ness and rivers in the desert."
Isaiah 43:15–19

Forget About It!

Forget the past. If you have trouble with
this concept, then just look ahead instead—
the view is better. God can change whatever
effect the past has had on you. Do not limit
your belief. Have faith in God.

I once taught a message about forgetting the past. During my preparation, the Holy Spirit inspired me with these thoughts: *Don't base anything or any way you think God might do things on your past experience. Look forward and think of the past as nonexistent.* Let's do that. Let's look to the future, trusting in God Almighty.

Good Things to Come?

God wants to bless you and is more than able to do so. Realize this.

> *Behold, this day I am going the way of all the earth. And you know in all your hearts and in all your souls that not one thing has failed of all the good things which the LORD your God spoke concerning you. All have come to pass for you; not one word of them has failed.*
> Joshua 23:14

*How beautiful upon the mountains
are the feet of him who brings good
news, Who proclaims peace,
Who brings glad tidings of good things,
Who proclaims salvation, Who says to
Zion, "Your God reigns!"* Isaiah 52:7

*I know the thoughts that I think toward
you, says the* LORD, *thoughts of peace
and not of evil, to give you a future and
a hope.* Jeremiah 29:11

*We know that all things work together
for good to those who love God, to those
who are the called according to His purpose.* Romans 8:28

*God is able to make all grace abound
toward you, that you, always having all
sufficiency in all things, may have an
abundance for every good work.*
2 Corinthians 9:8

What If You Have Misunderstood What God Is Doing in Your Life?

There are times when we don't understand what God is doing in our lives. We can't see the direction God is taking.

Have you ever thought people didn't like you because they ignored you, only to find out that they didn't even see you? You went through a ridiculous depression over the whole thing for no reason at all. This is similar to what can happen in our walk with God. Sometimes we misunderstand circumstances, leading us to misunderstand what God is doing.

Had Bad Effects from Bad Circumstances? What If God Can Help?

God can cause your feelings, thoughts, moods, and emotions to change. He can change your circumstances. Statements such as "God doesn't like me," "God has something against me," "God doesn't care," and "God let this terrible thing happen to me" are simply untrue. God loves you, and He is a good God. He can and will help.

What If God Didn't Do It?

Man's will and his own evil desires can be the cause of different circumstances and events. God is the One who can free you from the effects of your past.

God loves you. He will help you if you ask Him. God is moving by His Spirit the minute you ask in faith, in Jesus's name, believing in His promises. Just because you can't see what He is doing doesn't mean He isn't working.

> *As you do not know what is the way of the wind, or how the bones grow in the womb of her who is with child, so you do not know the works of God who makes everything.* Ecclesiastes 11:5

Think about what God can do! Your relationship with God is your greatest gift.

Nurture it. It will grow. Draw near to Him.
Walk with Him. Talk with Him.

9

A Close Walk with God

Four Keys

Draw near to God and He will draw near to you.
—James 4:8

Some years ago, the Lord gave me a message to teach. It was called "Four Keys to a Close Walk with God." I wanted to know how to safeguard my own spiritual life and began to seek the face of God for some answers. He gave me the message to help me as well as others. Here are those keys:

1. Put God and His Word first. Spend time in the Word and in prayer each day.

2. Have a healthy social life. You must have fun with other Christians. You need fellowship. Perhaps you can join a

Bible study at your church, through which you can make some friends. You need fun in your life.

3. Stay physically active. You need some sort of physical exercise or outlet. You need to attend to physical health—spiritual health and physical health are important.

4. Get involved in a ministry at your church. You need to get involved. You will feel stagnant if there is no outflow from your life. Be a blessing.

Learning to walk with God is our joy. I remember when I was born-again and enjoyed this new living reality of Christ in my life. I couldn't believe how awesome it was. I was attending Bible studies, meeting new friends there, and praying about everything. I read every recommended Christian book I could get my hands on. It was wonderful!

Then something happened. I didn't leave God and He didn't leave me, but I entered a season of dryness in my spiritual walk. I felt like I was in a desert. I was in an onslaught of temptation that previously had never existed in my life.

I talked to God about it. "What's going on, God? It feels like You are not there. There must be something more. Am I doing anything wrong?"

I didn't realize that these times happen to all of us. When asking other Christians about it, I often heard statements like "God wants you to learn to walk in faith." I have found that this is true. He wants us to know by faith that He cares.

God gave me the teaching "Four Keys to a Close Walk with God" out of my own need and a desire to know the truth about walking closely with Him.

Remember the four keys as a guideline to help you to stay spiritually on target with your relationship with God. Never get discouraged. Although life can get tough, you have the keys to victory!

10

The Last Prayer Secret

Praise and Worship God

Commit your way to the Lord, Trust also in Him, And He
shall bring it to pass.   —Psalm 37:5

After you've followed the simple steps, all
there is left to do is thank and praise God
for what He is doing in all you've prayed
about. Think of it! No need to worry, no
need to fret! It is God you are resting your
faith in. It is His promise that is the rock,
the foundation of your faith.

So, praise Him and thank Him. Enjoy
God. Realize and meditate on His beauty,
greatness, and glory! God never lies. You
can trust in Him. He is worthy of your

praise and adoration. You will definitely begin to see your prayers get answered.

Put time with God first in your life. Make room for Him. He loves you. He wants to spend time with you.

How do you get to know someone? How can you get closer to God? Draw near. He will be there.

When I first started out in a prayer time, it was ten minutes several times a day. I had heard how an hour was a good thing, and I couldn't conceive of what I could do for an hour. Pray about your prayer life. Ask God for what you would like it to be. Talk to him.

Years ago, I went through something that had filled me with disappointment and pain. I needed to keep the "good things" in mind. God gave me the words to a song. It is called "Trust in the Lord" and it goes like this:

Trust in the Lord

Words and music ©Susan Parr, ASCAP

Trust in the Lord
With all of your heart
And don't try to understand His ways.

Think of how Jesus
Is close beside you,
Living and walking with you every day.

Chorus

Think of the good things:
The power of God;
His abiding presence;
His wonderful love.
Think of the good things:
Have faith in God.
Walk with Him, talk with Him,
Have faith in God.

Come to the Lord
With all of your needs.

Trust Him with all the things of your heart.

His Word is eternal, unfailingly true.
Stand on it, walk in it
And He'll do His part.

11

Prayer Promises

Rest in God's Word

Commit your way to the Lord, Trust also in Him, And He
shall bring it to pass.   —Psalm 37:5

This chapter contains some of the promises I
trust in when I pray. I have also included
some others that have brought comfort to
my heart. I hope they will bless you as well.
My advice is to get a promises of God booklet
(available in Christian bookstores). There are
approximately seven thousand biblical
promises! It is fun to see all that belongs to
us as Christians.

Remember Jesus, All Powerful

Keeping your mind on Jesus and praying
about everything will bring great victory. Too

much emphasis has been placed on the devil, though it is still important to address this area. Be aware; be vigilant in prayer. Jesus is the big guy. The enemy is defeated. The

. Talking to the devil so much did not work for me. In fact, it left me a wreck, praying for hours and in constant fear. I was always afraid I had forgotten to say or command something. That was so wrong.

God is huge. In the Garden of Gethsemane, Jesus said that He could pray to His Father and that the Father would send Him legions of angels (Matthew 26:53). If you go through a time of trouble, pray to the Father in Jesus's name and ask Him to send His holy angels to fight. Even though Jesus made it so simple, that in no way diminishes the limitless power of God moving on our behalf when we pray to the Father in Jesus's name, rest in Him and His Word, and thank Him for what He is doing and will do.

The promises of God have the limitless power of God backing them. No need for formulas to get answers to prayer. The answer comes when you pray in line with God's Word. You will get results when you follow the scriptural principles in this book.

The Bible tells that all provisions and promises contained in His Word belong to you. "Peter opened his mouth and said: 'In truth I perceive that God shows no partiality' " (Acts 10:34). What God gave to Christians in the Bible, He gives to all Christians today.

Partakers of His Nature

We know that through the new birth we are indwelt by the Holy Spirit. The Holy Spirit *is* His divine nature. Think about that! Scripture says we are partakers of His divine nature!

His divine power has given to us all things that pertain to life and godliness, through the knowledge of Him who called us by glory and virtue, by which have been given to us exceedingly great and precious promises, that through these you may be partakers of the divine nature, having escaped the corruption that is in the world through lust. 2 Peter 1:3–4

Abide in God

If you abide in Me, and My words abide in you, you will ask what you desire, and it shall be done for you. John 15:7

This Book of the Law shall not depart from your mouth, but you shall meditate in it day and night, that you may observe to do according to all that is written in it. For then you will make your way prosperous, and then you will have good success. Joshua 1:8

[We] thank God without ceasing, because when you received the word of God which you heard from us, you welcomed it not as the word of men, but as it is in truth, the word of God, which also effectively works in you who believe. 1 Thessalonians 2:13

God Is Powerful

It is the Spirit who gives life; the flesh profits nothing. The words that I speak to you are spirit, and they are life. John 6:63

So shall My Word be that goes forth from My mouth; it shall not return to Me void, but it shall accomplish what I please, and it shall prosper in the thing for which I sent it. Isaiah 55:11

And what is the exceeding greatness of His power toward us who believe, according to the working of His mighty power which He worked in Christ when He raised Him from the dead… Ephesians 1:19–20

We are His workmanship, created in Christ Jesus for good works, which God prepared beforehand that we should walk in them. Ephesians 2:10

In Time of Trouble

He who has begun a good work in you will complete it until the day of Jesus Christ. Philippians 1:6

The Lord will deliver me from every evil work and preserve me for His heavenly kingdom. To Him be glory forever and ever. Amen!
2 Timothy 4:18

For Protection

No evil shall befall you, nor shall any plague come near your dwelling; for He shall give His angels charge over you, to keep you in all your ways.
Psalm 91:10–11

Promises for Answered Prayer

Be anxious for nothing, but in everything by prayer and supplication, with thanksgiving, let your requests be made known to God; and the peace of God, which surpasses all understanding, will guard your hearts and minds through Christ Jesus.
Philippians 4:6–7

Whatever you ask in My name, that I will do, that the Father may be glorified in the Son. If you ask anything in My name, I will do it. John 14:13–14

Most assuredly, I say to you, whatever you ask the Father in My name He will give you. Until now you have asked nothing in My name. Ask, and you will receive, that your joy may be full. John 16:23–24

All the promises of God in Him are Yes, and in Him Amen, to the glory of God through us. 2 Corinthians 1:2

Now to Him who is able to do exceedingly abundantly above all that we ask or think, according to the power that works in us, to Him be glory in the church by Christ Jesus to all generations, forever and ever. Amen. Ephesians 3:20–21

*My God shall supply all your need according to His riches in glory by Christ Jesus.*Philippians 4:19

This is the confidence that we have in Him, that if we ask anything according to His will, He hears us. And if we know that He hears us, whatever we ask, we know that we have the petitions that we have asked of Him. 1 John 5:14–15

Jesus's Words

When you pray, you shall not be like the hypocrites. For they love to pray standing in the synagogues and on the corners of the streets, that they may be seen by men. Assuredly, I say to you, they have their reward. But you, when you pray, go into your room, and when you have shut your door, pray to your Father who is in the secret place; and your Father who sees in secret will reward you openly. And when you pray, do not use vain repetitions as the heathen do. For they think that they will be heard for their many words. Therefore do not be like them. For your Father knows the things you have need of before you ask Him. In this manner, therefore, pray:

Our Father in heaven,
Hallowed be Your name.
Your kingdom come.
Your will be done
On earth as it is in heaven.
Give us this day our daily bread.
And forgive us our debts,
As we forgive our debtors.
And do not lead us into temptation,
But deliver us from the evil one.
For Yours is the kingdom and the power and the glory forever. Amen.